Little Book
O'Green Beans

Louise Pepper

authorHOUSE®

AuthorHouse™
1663 Liberty Drive
Bloomington, IN 47403
www.authorhouse.com
Phone: 1-800-839-8640

First published by AuthorHouse   2/28/2012

ISBN: 978-1-4685-5337-6 (e)
ISBN: 978-1-4685-5338-3 (sc)

Library of Congress Control Number: 2012903043

Printed in the United States of America

Preface

Once again my way to writing that *great novel* (it is started, and developing) I keep getting stalled in the land of food. The very staple of our existence. After the completion of the *Great Canadian Chicken* and *Of Borscht and Beyond*. I ran into a Bean and here is its story. In the land of great personal loves, next to the Arts and Creative Writing, I spend most of my Saturdays plotting the menus for the upcoming week for the household.

When my Goddaughter told me of her very productive green bean crop, my mind went back into a time when I had gardens, and one of the MOST prolific crops was indeed the **green bean**. **Phaseolus vulgaris** , Translated probably means, *Beans what Grow with great vigor* At least that is how I see it.

So, on the Saturdays of menus I began to explore some of many ways there are so serve, enjoy and be nourished by this humble little green tube like vegetable, a relative of the *Caragana* bush we saw edging our yards on the Canadian Prairies, I believe. I was amazed how very good it was, not only eat, but was also good for we humans.

There seems to be a never ending trail of ways to serve the bean with likely dozens more I have not yet found.

Do enjoy and try some of our culinary treasures. Bean up !

In Depth Nutritional Profile for Green beans

Description

While green beans are typically referred to as string beans, many varieties no longer actually feature the fibrous 'string' that runs down the length of the earlier varieties. Green beans are also commonly known as snap beans. *Haricots verts* are French green beans that are very thin and very tender.

Green beans are in the same family as shell beans, such as pinto beans, black beans and kidney beans. Yet unlike their cousins, green beans' entire bean, pod and seed, can be eaten.

Green beans range in size, but they usually average four inches in length. They are usually deep emerald green in color and come to a slight point at either end. They contain tiny seeds within their thin pods.

The scientific name for green beans is **Phaseolus vulgaris.**

History

Green beans and other beans, such are kidney beans, navy beans and black beans are all known scientifically as Phaseolus vulgaris. They are all referred to as "common beans," probably owing to the fact that they all derived from a common bean ancestor that originated in Peru. From there, they were spread throughout South and Central America by migrating Indian tribes. They were introduced to Europe around the 16h century by Spanish explorers returning from their voyages to the New World, and subsequently were spread through many other parts of the world by Spanish and Portuguese traders. Today, the largest commercial producers of fresh green beans include the United States, China, Japan, Spain, Italy and France.

How to Select and Store

If possible, purchase green beans at a store or farmer's market that sells them loose so that you can sort through them to choose the beans of best quality. Purchase beans that have smooth feel and a vibrant green color, and that are free from brown spots or bruises. They should have a firm texture and 'snap' when broken.

Store unwashed fresh beans pods in a plastic bag kept in the refrigerator crisper. Whole beans stored this way should keep for about three days.

How to Enjoy

Tips for Preparing Green Beans:

Just prior to using the green beans, wash them under running water. Remove both ends of the beans by either snapping them off or cutting them with a knife.

A Few Quick Serving Ideas:

Green beans are a classic ingredient in Salad Nicoise, a French cold salad dish that combines steamed green beans with tuna fish and potatoes. Healthy sauted green beans with shiitake mushrooms.

Prepare the perennial favorite, green beans almondine, by sprinkling slivered almonds on sauted beans.

Roast green beans, red peppers and garlic, and combine with olive oil and seasonings to make a delicious salad.

Add chopped green beans to breakfast frittatas.

In Depth Nutritional Profile for Green beans

Commonly referred to as string beans, the string that once was their trademark can seldom be found in modern varieties. Although these bright green and crunchy beans are available at your local market throughout the year, they are in season from summer through early fall when they are at their best and the least expensive.

Health Benefits

Green beans, while quite low in calories (just 43.75 calories in a whole cup), are loaded with enough nutrients to not only power up the Jolly Green Giant, but to put a big smile on his face. Green beans are an excellent source of vitamin C, vitamin K and manganese. Plus green beans are very good source of vitamin A (notably through their concentration of carotenoids including beta-carotene), dietary fiber, potassium, folate, and iron. Green beans are a good source of magnesium, thiamin, riboflavin, copper, calcium, phosphorous, protein, omega-3 fatty acids and niacin.

Cardiovascular Protection from Green Beans

For atherosclerosis and diabetic heart disease, few foods compare to green beans in their number of helpful nutrients. Green beans are a very good source of vitamin A, notably through their concentration of beta-carotene, and an excellent source of vitamin

C. These two nutrients are important antioxidants that work to reduce the amounts of free radicals in the body, vitamin C as a water-soluble antioxidant and beta-carotene as a fat-soluble one. This water-and-fat-soluble antioxidant team helps to prevent cholesterol from becoming oxidized. Oxidized cholesterol is able to stick to and build up in blood vessel walls, where it can cause blocked arteries, heart attack or stroke. Getting plenty of beta-carotene and vitamin C can help prevent these complications, and a cup of green beans will provide you with 16.6% of the daily value for vitamin A along with 20.2% of the daily value for vitamin C.

Green beans are also a very good source of fiber, a very good source of potassium and folate, and a good source of magnesium and riboflavin. Each of these nutrients plays a significant cardio-protective role.

Magnesium and potassium work together to help lower high blood pressure, while folate is needed to convert a potentially dangerous molecule called homocysteine into other, benign molecules (the riboflavin in green beans may also serve to protect against the build up of homocysteine in certain individuals). Since homocysteine can directly damage blood vessel walls if not promptly converted, high levels are associated with a significantly increased risk of heart attack and stroke. Lastly, fiber, which is also found in green beans, has been shown to lower high cholesterol levels. A cup of green beans supplies 16.0% of the daily value for fiber, 10.7% of the DV for potassium, 7.8% of the DV for magnesium, anmd 10.4% of the DV for folate. What this all adds up to is a greatly reduced risk of atherosclerosis, diabetic heart disease, heart attack, and stroke.

Colon Cancer Prevention

Green beans can also help prevent colon cancer. The vitamin C and beta-carotene in green beans help to protect the colon cells from the damaging effects of free radicals. Green beans' folate helps to prevent DNA damage and mutations in colon cells, even when they are exposed to cancer-causing chemicals. Studies show that people who eat foods high in vitamin C, beta-carotene, and/or folate are at a much lower risk of getting colon cancer than those who don't.

Green beans' fiber can help prevent colon cancer as well, as it has the ability to bind to cancer-causing toxins, removing them from the body before they can harm colon cells.

Anti-Inflammatory Nutrients

Beta-carotene and vitamin C both also have very strong anti-inflammatory effects. This may make green beans helpful for reducing the severity of diseases where inflammation plays a major role, such as asthma, osteoarthritis, and rheumatoid arthritis.

Green beans are a good source of riboflavin, which has been shown to help reduce the frequency of migraine attacks in people who suffer from them. Riboflavin's protective role in energy production may explain why. The oxygen-containing molecules the body uses to produce energy can be highly reactive and can inadvertently cause damage the mitochondria and even the cells themselves. In the mitochondria, such damage is largely prevented by a small, protein-like molecule called glutathione. Like many "antioxidant" molecules, glutathione must be constantly recycled, and it is vitamin B2 that allows this recycling to take place. (Technically, vitamin B2 is a cofactor for the enzyme glutathione reductase that reduces the oxidized form of glutathione back to its reduced version.) A cup of green beans supplies 7.1% of the DV for riboflavin.

Iron for Energy

Popeye was mistaken, green beans have almost twice as much iron as spinach. Green beans are a very good source of iron, an especially important mineral for menstruating women, who are more at risk for iron deficiency. Boosting iron stores with green beans is a good idea, especially because, in comparison to red meat, a well known source of iron, green beans provide iron for a lot less calories and are totally fat-free. Iron is an integral component of hemoglobin, which transports oxygen from the lungs to all body cells, and is also part of key enzyme systems for energy production and metabolism. And, if you're pregnant or lactating, your needs for iron increase. Growing children and adolescents also have increased needs for iron. In one cup of green beans, you'll be provided with 10.7% of the daily value for iron; a cup of spinach also provides a good amount of iron - 8.9% of iron's daily value.

Tuscan Green Beans

1 clove garlic, minced
¼ cup slivered salami (optional)
3 tablespoons olive oil
1 cup seeded and finely chopped tomato
2 tablespoons red wine vinegar
1 teaspoon oregano
Salt and pepper, to taste
1 pound fresh or frozen green beans

In medium saucepan, stir and cook garlic and salami in olive oil over medium heat until golden and crisp. Add tomato, vinegar, oregano, salt and pepper; stir until warm and blended. Remove from heat, cover and keep warm. Wash and trim fresh green beans. Boil, steam or microwave beans until tender and crisp, drain. Place on warm serving platter. Reheat sauce if necessary, spoon warm sauce over beans. Serve.

Pennsylvania Dutch Green Beans

3 slices bacon
1 small onion, sliced
2 teaspoons cornstarch
1/4 teaspoon salt
1/4 teaspoon dry mustard
1 (14.5 ounces) can cut Green Beans
1 tablespoon brown sugar
1 tablespoon vinegar
1 hard-cooked egg, chopped

Cook bacon in skillet until crisp; drain; crumble; reserve. Pour off all but 1 tablespoon of the bacon drippings. Add onion and saute until tender. Blend in cornstarch, salt and mustard. Drain beans, reserving 1/2 cup of liquid; stir reserved liquid into skillet. Cook, stirring constantly, until thickened and bubbly; stir in sugar and vinegar. Add beans. Heat all until bubbly hot. Sprinkle with crumbled bacon and egg.

Pickled Green Beans

A crunchy addition to any salad.

2 pounds green beans, fresh, trimmed

4 bulbs (to 8 bulbs) garlic, adjust to taste

4 sprigs dill, adjust to taste

1/4 cup salt

2 1/2 cups vinegar (cider or white) 2 1/2 cups water

1 teaspoon cayenne pepper (optional)

Place 1 to 2 heads (whole bulbs) of garlic and 1 to 2 sprigs of dill in hot pint jars. Pack beans lengthwise in hot jars, leaving 1/4-inch head space. Add cayenne pepper if desired.

Combine water, vinegar and salt. Bring to a full boil. Pour boiling mixture into jars filled with beans, leaving 1/4-inch head space. Wipe top edge of jar and place warmed lid on the jar. Add the band and tighten. Process 10 minutes in a boiling water bath. Remove and set on racks to cool. Do not set directly on a counter top after removing from hot water bath. may be placed on a towel Allow at least 2 weeks for flavors to develop before eating.

Garlic and Rosemary Green Beans recipe

1 pound Green Beans, frozen thawed

1/2 teaspoon Rosemary, dried

1/4 cup Olive oil

1/2 teaspoon Salt

1 clove Garlic crushed

Thaw green beans in a collander. Put olive oil, garlic, rosemary and salt in a skillet or stir-fry pan and mix. Add green beans. Stir-fry until beans are just softened. Serve immediately.

Cheese, Green Bean and Sesame Casserole

1 cup sesame seeds
2 cups green beans, trimmed and cut in half
1 onion, peeled and finely diced
2 tablespoons whole wheat flour
1/2 cup plain yogurt
1/2 cup dry white wine
1 cup grated cheese, Swiss or mozzarella (or a combination)
1 tablespoons butter

Preheat oven to 180°C/ 350°F. Heat a nonstick pan over medium heat and lightly toast the sesame seeds for 5 minutes.. Steam or lightly boil the beans until tender, but not soggy. Refresh under cold water. Toss with the diced onion, flour, salt, yogurt and wine. Grease and baking dish and turn the bean mixture into it. Spread the sesame seeds over the top and dot with butter. Bake for 30 minutes or until the top browns.

Oriental Sesame Green Beans

3 cups green beans, trimmed and cut into 1/2 inch pieces
2 tablespoons sesame seeds
2 tablespoons soy sauce
2 teaspoons oriental sesame oil
1/8 teaspoon nutmeg

Place green beans in a steamer basket over boiling water. Cover saucepan and steam 8 to10 minutes or until almost tender. Heat a heavy nonstick frying pan over medium high heat. Add sesame seeds. Shake skillet constantly until sesame seeds are golden. Reduce heat to medium low and stir in soy sauce, oil and nutmeg. Add green beans and toss. Serve.

Green Beans with Mushroom Butter

1 tablespoon unsalted butter, softened
5-1/2 oz mushrooms, minced
2 teaspoons fresh parsley, minced
2 cloves garlic, minced
1 lb green beans, trimmed

Combine first 4 ingredients and salt and pepper to taste in a bowl. Mix well. Place green beans in a steamer basket over boiling water. Cover pan and steam 10 to12 minutes or until tender. Transfer to a serving bowl and toss with mushroom butter.

Green Beans and Mushrooms and Sour Cream

2 cups green beans
1 Tbsp butter
2 cups fresh button mushrooms sliced
1 cup sour cream,
Salt and pepper to taste

Steam the beans until just tender and then drain well. Melt the butter in a large pan and saute the mushrooms on a high heat so that they do not lose their juices. Cook until tender. Stir in the beans and heat through. Add the sour cream and season with salt and pepper. Cook briefly but do not allow to boil. Serve mediately.

Green Bean & Potato Casserole

2 cans green beans, drained
1 can French fried onions
1/4 c. water
1 can condensed tomato soup
1 lb. ground meat
Grated Cheddar cheese (approx. 1 c.)
8 servings instant mashed potatoes
Salt & pepper

Brown ground meat and drain. In large casserole dish, combine ground beef, green beans, tomato soup, water, salt and pepper. Mix up the potatoes according to directions on the container and blend in 3/4 of the can of onion rings. Spread across top of green bean mixture. Bake for 25 minutes at 350 degrees. Top with the rest of the onion rings and grated cheese.

Baked Chicken with Beans & Apples

2-1/2 to 3 lb. chicken, cut up
1/2 tsp. salt
1/4 tsp. pepper
1 chicken bouillon cube
1/2 c. boiling water
1/2 c. apple juice
2 c. sliced fresh green beans, cut length wise on the pod.
1 c. diced peeled apples
1 tbsp. flour
1 tsp. ground cinnamon

Sprinkle both sides of chicken with salt and pepper. Place chicken on a rack in a shallow open roasting pan. Bake in hot oven (450 degrees) until browned, about 20 minutes. Reduce oven temperature to 350 degrees. Remove chicken and rack; pour off any fat from pan. Return chicken to pan. Dissolve bouillon in boiling water. Pour over chicken along with apple juice. Stir in green beans. Cover and bake 25 minutes. Stir in apple. Cover and bake 10 minutes longer. Meanwhile, in small saucepan mix flour with cinnamon. Blend with 1 tablespoon of cold water. Stir in hot pan liquid. Cook and stir until mixture boils and thickens slightly. Serve with chicken and vegetables.

Country Style Green Beans and Potatoes

1- 1/2 lbs. fresh green beans
8 slices bacon, quartered
1 sm. onion, chopped
5 c. water
1 tsp. salt
1/2 tsp. pepper
1-1/2 c. cubed red potatoes

Wash beans. Trim ends and remove strings. Cut into 1 1/2-inch slices; set aside. Fry bacon until crisp in a Dutch oven. Remove bacon and set aside. Saute onion in drippings until tender. Add water to cover. Bring to a boil; add bacon, beans, salt, pepper and return to a boil. Cover and simmer 15 minutes. Add potatoes and cook 10 minutes or until potatoes are tender. Drain. Yield: 6 servings.

Creamy Potato & Green Bean Salad

1/2 c. mayonnaise
1/3 c. milk
1 tbsp. prepared mustard
1/2 tsp. salt, or to taste
1/4 tsp. pepper, or to taste
3 c. diced cooked potatoes (2 lg.)
2 c. cooked, fresh or drained, canned cut green beans (8 oz.)
1 c. thin sliced celery
1/2 c. thinly sliced green onions
Romaine lettuce (optional)

In large bowl beat mayonnaise, milk, mustard, salt and pepper with a whisk or fork until blended. Add potatoes, green beans, celery and onions; fold gently until well coated with dressing. Cover and refrigerate least 2 hours. Leave in bowl or line a serving platter with romaine lettuce and spoon salad in center.

Green Bean and Veggie Bundles

1 med. carrot
1 med. zucchini
1 med. green pepper
1/4 lb. fresh green beans
6 egg roll skins, quartered
Cooking oil

Cut carrot, zucchini and green pepper into julienne strips. Cut green beans into 2-inch strips. Cook carrots and beans, covered, in boiling salted water for 5 minutes. Drain vegetables well. Using one quartered egg roll skin, place 4 vegetable strips in bundle below center of skin. Moisten edges of egg roll skin with water, roll up and press firmly to seal edges. Fry vegetable bundles a few at a time in deep fat for 3-4 minutes or until golden brown. Drain on paper toweling. Serve bundles warm with sauce. Makes 24 appetizers.

Sauce for Appetizers

Combine 1/2 cup sour cream, 1/2 cup mayonnaise and 2 tablespoons frozen orange juice concentrate, thawed and 1 teaspoon prepared mustard in a saucepan. Cook and stir over low heat until heated through; do not boil. Makes 1 cup.

Green Bean and Chicken Casserole

1 can French cut green beans, drained
1 c. sliced water chestnuts, drained
1 jar pimento, drained
1 can cream of celery soup
1/2 c. mayonnaise
1 onion, chopped
1 box long grain & wild rice with seasonings, uncooked
2 c. chicken or turkey cubes
2 c. chicken broth

Mix all of the above and spoon in a lightly greased 2 quart or layer casserole. Bake at 350 degrees for 45 minutes to 1 hour.

Green Bean and Corn Casserole

1 can French style green beans
1 can cream of celery soup
1/2 c. sour cream
1/2 c. chopped onion
1 can whole kernel corn
1/2 c. chopped fine celery
1 1/2 packs crushed crackers of choice
4 Tbsp. melted butter

Spray casserole dish with Cooking oil . Drain green beans and place in dish. Mix together cream of celery soup, sour cream, chopped onion, corn (drained) and chopped celery. Pour this mixture over the green beans. Place crushed crackers on top and pour melted butter over crackers. Bake 35 minutes on 350 or until brown.

Green Beans and Tomato

3/4 lb. fresh green beans
2 tsp. Dijon mustard
1/2 tsp. minced garlic
2 tbsp. red wine vinegar
4 tbsp. oil
1/8 tsp. ground cumin
2 tbsp. basil
3 red tomatoes, sliced
1/4 c. chopped onion

Trim off the ends of the beans. Drop them into boiling salted water to cover and cook until crisp tender, about 5 minutes. Do Not overcook. Drain and let cool. Place the mustard, garlic, and vinegar in a salad bowl. Gradually add the oil while stirring rapidly with a wire whisk. Add cumin and basil. Stir and blend. Add the green beans, tomatoes and onion. Toss and serve.

Green Beans with Mushrooms and Water Chestnuts

2 c. sliced fresh button mushrooms
1 tbsp. margarine
1/4 c. skim milk
1 tbsp. soy sauce
2 tsp. corn starch
1 tsp. seasoned salt
1 (16 oz.) can French-cut green beans, drained
1 (8 oz.) can sliced water chestnuts, drained

Combine mushrooms and margarine in 1-quart microwave-safe casserole. Cover with casserole lid. Microwave (high) for 3 to 4 minutes or until mushrooms are tender. Combine milk, soy sauce, corn starch, and salt; mix well. Stir into mushrooms. Microwave (high), uncovered, 2 to 3 minutes or until mixture boils and thickens, stirring once. Add green beans and water chestnuts. Mix lightly. Cover. Microwave (high) 4 to 6 minutes or until heated through, stirring once.

Green Bean Salad with Creamy Tarragon Dressing

Water
3 lb. green beans
1/2 c. mayonnaise
1/3 c. tarragon vinegar
1/4 tsp. salt
1 tsp. prepared mustard
1/2 tsp. pepper
1 med. red onion, thinly sliced

About 2 1/2 hours before serving: Place In a 4 quart saucepan over high heat 1 inch of boiling water, heat green beans to boiling. Reduce heat to low, cover and simmer 5-10 minutes until beans are tender crisp; drain. In a 13 x 9 inch baking dish, mix mayonnaise, vinegar, salt, mustard and pepper. Add green beans and onion; toss to coat with dressing. Cover and refrigerate 2 hours to blend flavors.

Green Bean Salad with Walnut Sauce

1 cooked potato, cut in chunks
2 c. green beans, cut in 1-inch
pieces, steamed
2 tbsp. virgin olive oil
3 tbsp. vinegar
1/2 tsp. salt
1/2 c. chopped walnuts
1 clove garlic, peeled
Dash cayenne pepper
1 tsp. ground coriander
3-4 tbsp. cold water
1/2 med. large white onion, cut in
1/2-inch pieces

Marinate potato and green beans in mixture of oil, 2 tablespoons vinegar and salt for 1/2 hour in refrigerator. Place walnuts, garlic, cayenne, coriander and 1 tablespoon vinegar in blender. Blend to paste, adding water until smooth. Use rubber spatula to force mixture down sides. Drain vegetables and stir in walnut sauce and onion. Chill for at least an hour before serving.

Hamburger Green Bean Casserole

1 can cream of mushroom soup
1/3 c. bread crumbs
1/4 c. onion, chopped
1 egg
1 lb. ground beef
Salt & pepper
2 cups Green Beans
3 cups Frozen Tater Tots of choice.

Mix 1/4 cup of the mushroom soup with the rest of the ingredients. Line a small casserole with this mixture like a pie shell. Mix remaining soup with 1 (16 ounce) can of green beans and fill centers of casserole. Top with crumbs or tater tots. Bake at 350 degrees for 35-40 minutes.

Herbed Green Beans

1 lb. fresh green beans
2 c. water
1/2 tsp. basil
1/2 tsp. marjoram
1 tbsp. fresh parsley
2 tbsp. chives
1/8 tsp. thyme
1 sm. onion, chopped
1 clove garlic, minced
2 tbsp. oil
1 tsp. salt
¼ tsp pepper

Cut off ends of green beans, wash and drain. Cook beans in 2 cups of boiling water, tightly covered for 10-15 minutes, until tender, but still crisp. Meanwhile, combine herbs in a small bowl. Then saute chopped onion and garlic in oil, adding the herbs toward the end. Add cooked beans to herb mixture, season to taste, toss lightly and serve.

Wieners, Potatoes and Green Bean Casserole

6-8 Wieners
7 to 8 small potatoes washed and (cubed)
1 can green beans
Onion

Boil cubed potatoes until soft. Boil hotdogs sliced in small circles. Saute onion in margarine in large skillet. Add potatoes, weiners and green beans. Mix and cook on low heat until desired consistency.

Lemon Green Beans

1 lb. fresh green beans
4 tbsp. minced onion
4 tbsp. butter, melted
2 tbsp. lemon juice
1/2 tsp. salt
1/4 tsp. pepper

Wash beans and remove strings. Cut beans into 1-1/2 inch pieces. Cook, covered, in a small amount of boiling water 12-15 minutes or until crisp-tender. Drain and set aside. Keep warm. Saute onion in butter until tender. Stir in lemon juice, salt and pepper. Add beans; cook 1 minute or until thoroughly heated, stirring constantly. Serve immediately.

Marinated Green Bean Salad

1 lb. fresh green beans
1 (2 oz.) jar sliced pimento, drained
1 med. tomato, chopped
1/2 c. chopped green pepper
1/2 c. reduced calorie Italian salad dressing
1/4 c. chopped fresh parsley
1/4 tsp. freshly ground pepper

Remove strings from green beans; wash thoroughly. Cut each bean lengthwise into 4 strips. Place in a steaming rack over boiling water. Cover and steam 5 minutes or until crisp-tender. Cool completely. Combine beans, pimento, tomato and green pepper in a shallow container. Combine salad dressing, parsley and pepper; stir well. Pour over bean mixture. Cover and refrigerate overnight. Yield: 6 servings (43 calories per serving).

Middle Eastern Green Bean Salad

1-1/2 lbs. green beans
1 clove garlic
Salt and pepper to taste
4-6 tbsp. lemon juice
1 sm. onion, finely chopped
2 tbsp. finely chopped parsley
4-6 tbsp. fine quality virgin olive oil

Wash and snap beans, into 2 inch lengths. Cook in salted water until tender but still crisp. Mash garlic and salt - add lemon juice and mix well. Add all other ingredients and toss. Best refrigerated at least an hour before serving. May be garnished with a few cherry tomatoes. Larger amounts of lemon and oil for a more tart salad

Marinated Mixed Vegetables

2 c. cut fresh green beans or 1 (9 oz.) pkg. frozen cut green beans or frozen Italian-style beans
1 c. fresh or frozen cauliflower flowerets
1 (2 oz.) jar sliced pimento, drained
1/4 c. reduced-calorie or oil-free
Italian salad dressing

Cook fresh green beans and cauliflower in a small amount of boiling water for 8 to 10 minutes or until crisp tender. (Or cook frozen green beans and cauliflower according to package directions, except omit salt.) Drain vegetables. Place in a mixing bowl. Add pimento and salad dressing. Toss until vegetables are coated. Cover and chill for 4 to 24 hours.

Potato / Green Bean Salad

6 cooked russet potatoes, peels on, chopped
2 hard boiled eggs, chopped
1/2 lb. bacon, cooked and crumbled
1 c. cooked green beans
1/4 chopped onion
1/2 c. chopped celery
1/2 c. each whole ripe and green olives

Toss all ingredients together. Blend with dressing.

DRESSING:
1/4 c. mayonnaise
2 tbsp. Dijon mustard
1/4 c. tarragon-flavored vinegar or rice wine vinegar
1 tbsp. dill weed
Salt to taste
1/4 c. minced fresh parsley Mix together. plate and serve.

Sauteed Green Beans

1-1/2 lbs. fresh green beans
Wash & break beans into 1" pieces. Place in 2 quart casserole.
1/4 c. margarine or butter
1/2 tsp. salt
1/4 tsp. savory leaves
1/8 tsp. oregano
1/8 tsp. pepper

Melt margarine, add seasonings and pour over beans. Toss to coat beans. Cover. microwave at High for 9 to 13 minutes, stirring once. Cover, let stand 3 minutes.

Spanish Green Beans

3-3/4 c. fresh green beans
1 medium onion, chopped
2 tbsp. reduced calorie margarine
1-1/2 tsp. salt
1/2 tsp. garlic powder
1/4 tsp. pepper
5 med. tomatoes, diced and seeded
2 med. green peppers, seeded and chopped

Cut beans into 1 1/2 inch pieces; wash thoroughly and drain. Saute onion in margarine in nonstick skillet until tender. Add beans, salt, garlic powder and pepper. Cover and continue to cook over low heat for 10 minutes, stirring frequently. Stir in tomatoes and green pepper. Cover and simmer 25-30 minutes or until beans are tender.

Tuna Green Bean Casserole

1 lg. can green beans (drained)
1 can water packed tuna
1 can mushrooms pieces drained
2 tbsp. dried onion flakes
3 cheese slices

In mixing bowl, mix tuna, green beans, and onion flakes. Add cut up mushrooms. Mix well. Have individual casseroles; divide into 3 to 4 casseroles. Top each casserole with 1 slice of cheese. Bake in oven until cheese has melted.

Turkey Green Bean Casserole

2 c. cooked, diced turkey breast
1 can French cut green beans, drained
1 c. cooked white rice
1 c. cooked long wild rice
1 can cream of celery soup
1/4 c. mayonnaise
1/2 c. sliced water chestnuts
2 tbsp. chopped pimiento
1/4 tsp. salt

Mix all of ingredients together. Bake at 350 degrees for about 30 minutes.

Country Beans

10 ounces minced bacon
1 medium onion, julienne
1 pound fresh snap beans
24 ounces chicken stock
1 tablespoon butter
*salt and pepper

Directions
Saute bacon and onions in a medium sauce pan on medium heat.

Then add snap beans, stock, and butter.

Cover with a lid and cook until beans are tender.

Add salt and pepper to taste and serve.

French Bean Casserole

1 tablespoon extra virgin olive oil,
1 small onion, minced
6 ounces crimini mushrooms, sliced
1 can condensed cream of mushroom soup,
1 cup heavy cream
1 pound baby green beans, trimmed and cleaned
1/2 cup toasted almonds

Preheat: oven to 350 degrees F In a medium skillet over medium heat, heat oil.

Add onion and saute until soft. Stir in mushrooms.

Increase heat to medium-high and saute until mushrooms are golden and most of the moisture has evaporated.

Stir in soup and cream. Cook and stir until simmering.

Stir in the green beans. Pour mixture into a buttered 9x13-inch baking dish and top with toasted almonds

Bake for 20 to 25 minutes or until beans are tender.

Green Beans Saute

In this dish, green beans and onions are lightly saute in just 1 tablespoon of oil.

1 lb fresh or frozen green beans, cut in 1-inch pieces
1 Tbsp vegetable oil
1 large yellow onion, halved lengthwise, thinly sliced
1/2 tsp salt
1/8 tsp black pepper
1 Tbsp fresh parsley, minced

If using fresh green beans, cook in boiling water for 10 or 12 minutes or steam for 2 or 3 minutes until barely fork tender. Drain well. If using frozen green beans, thaw first. Heat oil in large skillet. Sauté onion until golden. Stir in green beans, salt, and pepper. Heat through.

Before serving, toss with parsley.

Green Beans and Cabbage

4 tablespoons butter
3 cups chopped cabbage
1 1/2 cups fresh cut green beans
1 teaspoon ground coriander

Directions
In large skillet, melt butter over medium-high heat for 3 to 4 minutes, until butter begins to turn golden brown. Remove from heat and add cabbage and green beans; toss to coat with butter.

Sprinkle in coriander and toss well.

Return to stove and cook over low heat, covered, 10 to 15 minutes, until vegetables are crisp-tender, stirring occasionally.

Green Beans with Coconut

2 pounds fresh green beans
1 tablespoon butter
1 teaspoon mustard seed
2 teaspoons coriander seed
1/2 cup finely chopped onion
1 teaspoon grated fresh ginger
2 teaspoons salt
1/2 cup flaked coconut
Dash hot pepper sauce

Directions
Clean green beans, slice into 2-inch pieces and set aside.

In large skillet melt butter over medium-high heat.

Saute mustard seed, coriander seed, onion and ginger for 1 minute.

Stir in beans and salt.

Stir-fry for about 5 minutes, until beans are still crisp.

Stir in coconut and hot pepper sauce.

Cover, lower heat and cook for about 10 minutes, until beans are tender.

Green Beans with Glazed Onions

2 16-ounce bags frozen pearl onions, thawed
1/2 cup balsamic vinegar, divided
2 tablespoons butter
2 tablespoons vegetable oil
1 teaspoon dried thyme
1 teaspoon ground black pepper
1 teaspoon salt, divided
3 pounds fresh green beans, cleaned and trimmed
3 tablespoons olive oil
1 tablespoon stone-ground mustard
1 1/2 teaspoon sugar

Directions

In medium saucepan, combine onions, 4 tablespoons vinegar, butter, vegetable oil, thyme, pepper and 1/2 teaspoon salt. Heat over low heat until butter is melted; stirring to coat onions.

Place mixture on a baking sheet and roast in a 400 degree F oven for 35-40 minutes, stirring occasionally until onions are browned; remove from oven and set aside. Blanch green beans in large saucepan of boiling water just until tender, about 5 minutes. Drain and rinse with cold water; set aside.

In small bowl, whisk together olive oil, mustard, sugar, the remaining 4 tablespoons of the vinegar, and the remaining 1/2 teaspoon of salt. In a large bowl, toss the dressing together with the onions and the green beans. Place the mixture in a large casserole dish and cover.

Bake for 20 minutes in a 350 degree F oven.

Green Beans & Leeks with Hazelnuts

Boiling salted water in 2 pans
2 lbs. fresh green beans
4 leeks white portions only throuoghly washed, then sliced
4 tablespoons butter
3/4 cup hazelnuts, toasted and chopped
1/2 teaspoon lemon juice

Trim off ends of beans and slice diagonally in 2" pieces

Trim outer leaves of leeks and slice into 2" diagonal pieces.

Cook in separate pots 7 to 10 minutes or until tender-crisp.

Drain and rinse with cold water to stop cooking.

Melt butter in large frying pan and add beans, leeks, and hazelnuts.

Saute until heated through, sprinkle with lemon juice, season with salt and pepper if desired.

Spicy Snap Beans

1 teaspoon sesame oil
1 tablespoon olive oil
1 sweet onion, julienne
1 jalapeno, minced
1 pound snap beans, washed and snapped
1 teaspoon chili powder
2 tablespoons garlic, minced
1/4 cup sodium-free soy sauce

Directions
Place a large saute pan on medium-high heat. Add sesame oil, olive oil, onion, and jalapeno.

Cook for 2 minutes. Then add beans, chili powder, garlic, and soy sauce.

Cover and cook for 5 minutes. Serve immediately.

Dry-fried Green Beans with Hoisin Sauce and Garlic

1 cup vegetable oil, for shallow frying
2 cups green beans

For the sauce
2 large red chillies
1.5 tbsp hoisin sauce
1 garlic clove, finely chopped
1/4 tsp sea salt
1/4 tsp vegetable oil

Method
Heat the oil in a hot wok or deep pan set over a high heat.

Fry the beans for 1- 2 minutes, until just tender and slightly wilted. Remove from the oil, drain on paper towel and set aside.

Cut the chillies in half lengthways and scrape out the seeds.

Carefully empty the hot oil from the wok/pan and wipe it clean with paper towel. Combine the hoisin sauce, garlic, salt and oil in the cleaned pan/wok

Stir in the chillies.

Toss the cooked beans into the sauce and stir-fry for 2 to 3 minutes, coating them in the sauce. Serve at once.

Green Beans with Tahini and Garlic

This green bean dish combines garlic and sesame seed paste (tahini) giving it a very unique taste

2 -1/2 lbs green beans (fresh or frozen)
1 teaspoon salt or to taste
6 Tablespoon grape seed cooking oil
2 teaspoon mustard seeds
8-9 garlic cloves, crushed
1" piece ginger, shredded
3 Tablespoon tahini (seasame seed paste)
4 Tablespoon fresh cilantro, chopped
1/4 teaspoon black pepper
1/4 teaspoon cayenne pepper
1 Tablespoon lemon juice

Method:
Cut beans 1" long. Steam until crisp and tender. Heat oil on medium heat, add mustard seeds. When they pop turn heat low and add garlic and ginger. Add rest of ingredients. Mix well and heat through. Serve warm.

This dish is quick and easy and accompanies any food. It's light in taste, but at the same time full in flavor.

Green Beans & Carmelized Sweet Onions

1 pound green beans
1 medium red bell pepper -- cut into juliennes
Grape Seed oil
1/2 pound sweet onions whole peeled
2 teaspoons sugar
1 teaspoon dried oregano
salt and pepper -- to taste
2 tablespoons balsmic vinegar

Directions
Blanch the onions in a large pot of boiling for about a minute. Remvove the onions to an ice bath. Now blanch the green beans in the same water for about 5 minutes. Remove the beans to the ice bath. This will set the nice green color and stop the cooking.

Place 1 tablespoon of oil in a sauce pan and heat until the oil starts to shimmer and just starts to smoke. Place the onions in the saute pan. Season with salt and pepper. Reduce the heat to medium high and cook t onions until they start to brown. Add the sugar to help with this carmelization. Once the onions are nicely carmelized, remove them from the pan.

Add the green beans and red peppers to the pan and saute for about 4 - 5 minutes. Add the onions back in and drizzle a the balsamic vinegar over the veggies. Season with salt and pepper and serve.

Green Beans With Toasted Pecans and Blue Cheese

Serving Size : 2

1/2 teaspoon Dijon mustard
2 teaspoons cider vinegar
1 tablespoon minced shallots
1 teaspoon minced fresh tarragon or Italian parsley
2 1/2 tablespoons olive oil -- extra-virgin preferred
1 tablespoon vegetable oil
1/2 cup pecan halves
Salt to taste
3/4 pound green beans -- cut into 1-inch
lengths on diagonal
2 ounces blue cheese -- crumbled

Whisk mustard, vinegar, shallots and tarragon in small bowl or 4-cup measuring cup. Whisk in olive oil. Set aside. In small, deep skillet, heat vegetable oil on high heat. Add pecans; saute until pecans brown, stirring frequently. Drain on paper towel and season with salt. Coarsely chop.

In large saucepan, bring about 6 cups of water to rapid boil on high heat. Add beans; cook until beans are tender-crisp, 3-6 minutes, depending on thickness of beans. Drain and refresh with cold water. Toss beans with vinaigrette. Add cheese and nuts; toss. Taste and adjust seasoning.

Pancetta Green Beans

12 ounces green beans, trimmed
3 ounces pancetta,* coarsely chopped
1 tablespoon butter

Cook beans in large pot of boiling salted water until crisp-tender, about 4 minutes. Drain. Transfer to bowl of ice water; cool 5 minutes. Drain. Transfer beans to paper towels and pat dry.

Heat large skillet over medium heat. Add pancetta and saute until crisp, about 3 minutes. Using slotted spoon, transfer to paper-towel-lined plate to drain. Increase heat to medium-high. Add butter to same skillet. Add beans and stir until heated through, about 4 minutes. Season with salt and pepper. Stir in pancetta.

*Pancetta (Italian bacon cured in salt) is available at Italian markets and in the refrigerated deli case of many supermarkets.

Green Bean Quickie

1 can green beans (french/cut)
1 tablespoon cornstarch
1 tablespoon lemon juice
1 ounce processed cheese or 2 slices American cheese
salt and pepper

Open can and leave lid on.Drain juice from can into a small sauce pan .Add cornstarch and stir.

Add cheese. Turn on heat to boiling, stir constantly.When thick and bubbly add green beans.

Add lemon,salt,and pepper. Stir check seasoning. Serve.

Authentic Hungarian Green Beans

(Kapros zoldbabfozelek)

Hungarian style green beans are unusual in that it combines, ingredients that make a dish that is sweet, sour, and dilly. This could only come from Hungary, where variety of taste in a meal is commonplace. Use fresh or frozen cut green beans for this dish. Not canned!

2 packages of green beans
2 Tbl. shortening or butter
2 Tbl. flour
1/2 cup of sliced Red onion
1/4 cup of rice vinegar
2 tsp. sugar
1 Tbl. chopped fresh dill

Cook beans in salted water till tender, not soft. Melt shortening or butter, add onions and saute till limp, add chopped dill. Then add flour making a roux. Add 1 cup of water, the sugar and vinegar and stir while the sauce gets thick as it is heated. Add drained beans, and mix, if too thick add a little more water.

Green Beans & Peppers

16 ounces green beans, cooked
1 each red, yellow or orange bell pepper, sliced in strips
1 small onion, halved and sliced
2 cloves garlic, minced
2 tablespoons butter
salt and pepper to taste

Directions:
Melt butter in a large skillet over medium-low heat. Add green beans, peppers, onion, and garlic. Cook slowly, stirring, until peppers are crisp tender, about 8 to 10 minutes. Add salt and pepper to taste

Green Bean and Cheese Casserole

3 cups cooked and drained green beans (reserve ½ c liquid) (use canned, or fresh cooked)
2 tablespoons butter
3 tablespoons flour
1 cup milk
1/2 cup shredded cheese
1 tablespoon prepared mustard
1/2 cup liquid from drained green beans
1/8 teaspoon pepper
1/2 teaspoon salt
1/4 cup bread crumbs tossed with 1 tablespoon melted butter

Cook rare beans; drain and reserve 1/2 cup of liquid (Heat through if using canned beans). Melt 2 tablespoons butter in a saucepan; blend in flour. Add milk slowly and cook until thickened, stirring constantly. Add cheese, mustard, and reserved cooking liquid. Stir until cheese melts. Add salt and pepper. Place alternating layers of green beans and sauce in a greased casserole, then top with buttered crumbs. Bake at 350° for 30 minutes.

Sweetened Green Beans & Cream

* 4 to 5 cups cut green beans
* 2 tablespoons finely chopped onion
* 1/4 cup chopped fresh parsley
* 3 tablespoons butter
* 1/4 cup flour
1 cup liquid from cooked beans
salt to taste
2 teaspoons sugar
3 tablespoons vinegar
1 cup sour cream

Cook green beans in boiling salted water until tender. Drain, reserving 1 cup of the cooking liquid. In a saucepan, heat butter over low heat; add onion and parsley and saute until tender. Blend in flour; stir, adding reserved 1 cup liquid from beans, salt, sugar, and vinegar.

Add beans and heat through. Just before serving add sour cream. Heat just until hot; do not boil.

Basil Green Beans

1 pound green beans, washed and trimmed (about 3 cups trimmed)
1 tablespoons olive oil
1 tablespoon butter
1 clove garlic, cut in half
1 tablespoon chopped onion
1- 1/2 teaspoons salt
1 teaspoon dried leaf basil, crumbled
1/2 teaspoon sugar
1/8 teaspoon pepper
1/4 cup boiling water

Cut green beans in halves. Heat oil and butter in a skillet; saute onion and garlic until softened. Remove garlic from the skillet. Add green beans, salt, basil, sugar, pepper, and boiling water.

Cover and cook over medium heat until tender, about 20 minutes. Add a little more water, if necessary.

Grilled Green Bean & Eggplant Salad

2 Japanese eggplants
1/2 lb fresh green beans, whole
1/4 cup balsamic vinegar
2 large red bell peppers, julienned
2 cups mixed greens
2 tbsp minced red onion
1 tbsp olive oil
2 tbsp lemon juice
2 tbsp balsamic vinegar
salt & pepper

Slice eggplants into rounds 1/4" thick. Toss with green beans in balsamic vinegar. Grill 8 to 10 minutes, turning frequently.

In a large salad bowl, toss together bell peppers, greens, onions, live oil, lemon juice & 2 tbsp balsamic vinegar. Add salt & pepper. Arrange grilled vegetables on top. Serve immediately.

Shanghai Stir-Fried String Beans

1 lb fresh green beans
2 teaspoons sesame seeds
1 tablespoon sugar
2 tablespoons rice wine vinegar
1/4 teaspoon white pepper
2 teaspoons light soy sauce
1/2 teaspoon sesame oil
2 1/2 tablespoons vegetable oil
1/2 teaspoon salt

Trim, wash and parboil beans for 2 minutes in rapidly boiling water. Drain and rinse with cold water. Heat sesame seeds in a dry frying pan over moderate heat. Remove when seeds begin to pop. Combine the sugar, rice wine vinegar, white pepper, soy sauce, and sesame oil for the seasoning mixture.

Put a wok/pan on very high heat. When very hot, add oil, salt and then the beans and stir-fry for 1 minute. Add the seasoning mixture and stir-fry for another minute. Add sesame seeds and blend well. Transfer to a heated serving platter.

Green Beans in Black Bean Sauce

1 lb fresh green beans
2 tbsp black bean paste
2 tbsp low sodium soy sauce or tamari
1/4 cup cold water
1 tbsp corn starch

Wash green beans and trim into bite sized pieces. Steam or microwave with a little water until just tender-crisp. Drain and rinse with cold water to stop cooking process. Mix together the black bean paste, soy sauce, water and corn starch until very smooth.Heat a wok or large saucepan to medium high. Add some water and the cooked beans. When beans are heated (about 2 minutes) add the sauce. Stir constantly to coat the beans (sauce will get very thick). Serve immediately over hot cooked rice.

Louisiana Green Beans

1 lb fresh green beans
2 cups tomatoes, diced
1/2 cup chopped celery
1/4 cup chopped seeded green bell pepper
1/2 teaspoon onion powder

Cook beans until tender, then add remaining ingredients and cook over medium heat until cooked through, about 15 minutes.

White & Green Bean Soup

1 1/2 cups dried white beans, Great Northern, navy, or baby lima
6 cups water
3 cloves garlic, chopped
2 tsp salt
4 cups beef broth
1/4 tsp freshly ground black pepper
1 tsp fresh rosemary, crumbled
2 cups fresh green beans (about 3/4 lb), cut on the diagonal in 1-inch pieces
1 tbsp butter
Juice of 1/2 lemon

Wash and pick over the dried beans. Put them into a large saucepan or kettle with the water and bring to a boil. Remove from the heat, cover, and allow to stand for 1 hour.

Return to the heat and bring to a boil again. Reduce heat and simmer, partially covered, for 1/2 hour. Using a heavy fork, mash the garlic with the salt until no large chunks remain. Add to the saucepan with the beans. Add the broth, pepper, and rosemary. Simmer, partially covered, until beans are tender. This can take 15 minutes or as long as 1 hour; timing for beans is hard to predict -- keep checking.

Cook the green beans uncovered in 2 quarts of boiling salted water until they are tender-crisp and bright green. Drain and add to the soup when the white beans are tender but not mushy. If green beans are not to be added right away, rinse in cold water to retain color. Stir in the butter and lemon. Serve at once, while green beans are still bright. Soup can be made ahead to this point, and refrigerated or frozen after thorough cooling.

Note: If you want some of the soup pureed, do it before adding the green beans -- the color will be better.

Impossible Green Bean Pie

8 oz fresh green beans, cut lengthwise into strips
1 1/2 cups milk
4 oz can mushrooms, stems and pieces, drained
3/4 cup Bisquick Baking Mix
1/2 cup onion, chopped
3 eggs
2 garlic cloves, crushed
1 tsp salt
1 cup cheddar cheese, shredded
1/4 tsp pepper

Heat oven to 400 degrees. Grease a 10 inch pie plate. Heat beans and 1 inch salted water (1/2 teaspoon salt to 1 cup water) to boiling. Cook uncovered 5 minutes. Cover and cook until tender, 5 to 10 minutes; drain. Mix beans, mushrooms, onion, garlic and cheese in plate. Beat remaining ingredients until smooth, 15 seconds in blender on high or 1 minute with hand beater. Pour into plate.

Bake until knife inserted between center and edge comes out clean, 30 to 35 minutes. Cool 5 minutes.

Old-Fashioned Green Beans

6 bacon strips cut in half
2 lbs fresh green beans
3 tablespoons brown sugar
1/2 cup water

In a large skillet, cook bacon over medium heat until crisp-tender, about 5 minutes. Add beans, brown sugar and water. Stir gently; bring to a boil. Reduce heat; cover and simmer for 15 minutes or until beans are crisp-tender. Remove to a serving bowl with a slotted spoon.

Dilled Pasta Salad with Green Beans

DRESSING
1/3 cup white wine vinegar
1 tbsp olive oil, extra light
1 tsp dill weed
1/4 tsp salt
1/4 tsp dry mustard
1/8 tsp pepper

SALAD
5 oz (2 cups) rotini pasta
1 cup sliced carrots
1 cup cut 1" fresh green beans
1/2 cup red bell pepper strips
4 green onions, sliced (1/2 cup)
8 cherry tomatoes, quartered
1/2 cup sliced cucumber
3 oz cubed low fat mozzarella cheese (1/2 cup)

In a jar, combine all dressing ingredients, and shake well. Cook pasta in 3 quarts boiling water to desired doneness, adding carrots and green beans during the last 2-4 minutes or pasta cooking time. Drain. Rinse thoroughly with cold water to cool rapidly. In a large serving bowl, combine cooled pasta mixture and remaining salad ingredients. Pour dressing over salad; toss gently.

Brown Rice Pilaf with Vegetables & Garlic

1 tbsp olive oil
1 cup chopped onion
1 1/2 cups brown rice
8 large garlic cloves, pressed
3 cups water
1 tsp salt
1 cup fresh green beans, cut into 2-inch pieces
1 cup yellow crookneck squash, cubed
1 cup broccoli florets
1 cup fresh corn kernels or frozen, thawed
1/3 cup chopped red bell pepper
1 tbsp sesame seeds, toasted
2 tsp light soy sauce

Heat oil heavy large skillet over low heat. Add onion; saute until golden and tender, about 10 minutes. Add rice and garlic; saute 1 minute. Add 3 cups water and salt; bring to boil. Reduce heat to low, cover tightly and cook until rice is tender and almost all liquid is absorbed, about 35 minutes; do not stir. Uncover skillet and place green beans, squash, broccoli, corn and carrot evenly over surface of rice. Cover and cook until vegetables are crisp-tender, about 10 minutes. Remove from heat. Stir in red bell pepper and sesame seeds. Mix in soy sauce. Toss to coat.

Tropical Green Beans

4 tbsp olive oil
1 lb fresh green beans, cleaned, cut and dried
1 small yellow onion, cut into rings
6 cloves garlic, peeled and halved
1/2 tsp salt
2 tbsp balsamic vinegar
3 stalks hearts of palm, cut into 1/2" rings
1/3 cup diced sun-dried tomatoes, packed in oil
2 tsp toasted pine nuts
freshly ground black pepper

Preheat oven to 400 degrees F. Brush a large baking dish with 2 tablespoons of the olive oil. Put green beans, onion, and garlic in dish, drizzle with remaining oil and sprinkle with salt. Bake for 25 minutes, stirring beans at least 3 times. When tender, remove beans from oven and transfer to bowl. Immediately drizzle with vinegar. Add hearts of palm, tomatoes, pine nits and pepper to taste and toss.

Dilled Green Beans & New Potatoes

1/2 lb small new potatoes, quartered
1/2 lb fresh green beans, trimmed, broken into 2" pieces
1/4 cup nonfat sour cream
2 tablespoons chopped fresh dill weed
1/8 teaspoon salt
dash pepper
1/2 teaspoon olive oil
1 clove garlic, minced

In medium saucepan, bring about 2 cups water to a boil. Add potatoes and green beans; return to a boil. Reduce heat; cover and simmer 9-11 minutes or until beans are crisp-tender. Meanwhile, in a small bowl, combine all remaining ingredients; blend well. Drain vegetables; rinse with cold water to cool slightly. Place in serving bowl. Add sour cream mixture, toss to coat. Serve immediately or refrigerate until serving time.

Minted Green Beans with Red Onion

2 pounds green beans, trim, snap into inch long pieces add 1/4 cup olive oil
1 teaspoon Dijon-style mustard 3 tablespoons minced fresh mint leaves
1 tablespoon white-wine vinegar 1/2 cup finely chopped red onion
Salt and pepper to taste

In a kettle of boiling water cook the beans for 2 to 4 minutes, or until they are crisp-tender. Transfer them with a slotted spoon to a bowl of ice and cold water to stop the cooking, and drain them well. Pat the beans dry with paper towels and chill them, covered, for at least 3 hours or overnight.

In a large bowl whisk together mustard, vinegar, and salt and pepper to taste, add oil in a stream, whisking, and whisk dressing until it is emulsified. Add beans, mint, and onion and toss mixture until it is combined well.

Basil Buttered Green Beans

2 cups fresh green beans, cut into 2-inch pieces
2 tbsp. onion, chopped
2 tbsp. celery, chopped
1/4 cup water
1 tsp. butter buds or butter, melted
1-1/2 tsp. fresh basil, minced or 1/2 tsp. dry
1/4 tsp. salt
1/8 tsp. pepper

In a saucepan, combine beans, onion, celery and water. Cover and cook for 5 minutes or until beans are tender. Drain. Add the butter, basil, salt and pepper; stir to coat. Serve immediately.

Dilly Green Beans

1 pkg. (10 oz.) frozen green beans
1/3 cup dairy sour cream
1 tsp. instant minced onion
1 tsp. dill weed or 1/2 tsp. dill seed
1/2 tsp. salt
1 dash pepper

Prepare green beans as directed on package. Drain . Add remaining ingredients. Toss lightly to blend well.

Festive Green Beans

1 lb. fresh green beans or 1 can (16 oz.) green beans
1/2 tsp. salt (optional)
1/4 tsp. pepper
1/2 tsp. garlic powder
3/4 can Mexican stewed tomatoes
1/2 cup water

Cut fresh beans into half; place in a saucepan. Add water and salt. Bring to a boil. Reduce heat and simmer 15 minutes or until tender; drain. Add the pepper, garlic powder and tomatoes; heat through.

Bacon Fried Beans

3 slices bacon
1 can (16 oz.) drained whole or cut green beans
1/2 tsp. salt
1/8 tsp. pepper

Directions:
In a medium saucepan, fry bacon until crisp. Drain on paper towel, reserving bacon drippings. To reserved drippings, add remaining ingredients. Cook over medium heat about 5 mintues, stirring occasionally, until heated through. Sprinkle with crumbled bacon.

Green Beans Mushrooms and Almonds

1 tbsp. olive oil
2 to 3 cloves garlic
6 lg. button mushrooms, sliced
1/2 to 3/4 cup whole almonds (more or less to taste and to fit your dieting goals)
1/2 lb. frozen French style green beans
Soy sauce, to taste

Heat oil over medium heat. Saute garlic until soft, being careful not to let it burn. Add sliced mushrooms and

German-Style Green Beans

1 lb. fresh green beans, trimmed
4 oz. country bacon, sliced
3 to 4 shallots, minced
Red wine vinegar
Bacon drippings (if needed)
Brown sugar
Salt and pepper (to taste)

Steam beans until tender (about 16-18 minutes in my steamer) or cook by another method. Fry bacon until crisp and set aside; cut or crumble into small pieces. Cook minced shallot if bacon drippings (adding more if needed) until tender and lightly browned. Add several tablespoons of vinegar to pan, and sweeten to taste with brown sugar or twin (should have a pleasant sweet-sour balance). Add cooked beans to pan along with crisp bacon, and season to taste with salt and pepper. Simmer over low heat, stirring often, until sauce dissipates. Serve hot.

Green Beans Braised with Mint and Potatoes

3 tbsp. *total* olive oil and margarine, mixed
1 cup tomato sauce
1 lb. fresh green beans, trimmed and cut 1 inch pieces
1 tbsp. fresh parsley, chopped (optional)
2 md. potatoes, peeled and sliced
Salt and freshly ground pepper, to taste
Fresh mint, chopped, to taste

Heat the fat in pan and mix in the tomato sauce. Add the green beans and parsley to the pan with enough water to almost cover. Tuck the potato slices in between, partially cover the pan, and simmer for 25 minutes, stir and season with salt, pepper, and 2 tablespoons chopped mint. Cook uncovered until the beans and potatoes are fork tender, about 10 more minutes. If the sauce has not thickened, pour it into a small pan, and boil down to one cup, then combine with the beans and potatoes in a warm serving bowl.

Green Beans Tarragon

2 cups cooked green beans
1/4 cup salad oil
1/4 cup tarragon or cider vinegar
1/4 tsp. tarragon
Lettuce leaves

Combine green beans, oil, vinegar and tarragon in a bowl. Chill in the refrigerator for 20 minutes or until ready to serve. To serve, spoon beans and dressing over lettuce leaves on individual serving dishes.

Green Beans Tossed with Herbs

1 cup green beans, frozen
2 tbsp. corn oil
1 tsp. rosemary, crushed
1 tsp. basil
Salt and pepper

Cook green beans in water until tender. Drain and toss beans with oil and herbs. Serve hot.

Old Fashioned Green Beans

6 slices bacon, cut in 1/2-inch pieces
2 lb. fresh green beans
3 tbsp. brown sugar
1/2 cup water

In a large skillet, cook bacon over medium heat until crisp-tender, about 5 minutes. Add beans, brown sugar and water. Stir gently; bring to a boil. Reduce heat; cover and simmer for 15 minutes or until beans are crisp-tender. Remove to a serving bowl with a slotted spoon.

Onion Simmered Green Beans

1 can (16 oz.) undrained whole green beans
1 to 2 tbsp. dry onion soup mix

Directions:
Place undrained beans in a small saucepan. Add onion soup mix. Heat through. Drain liquid and serve.

Sesame Green Beans

(Chinese green bean stir fry)

1 lb. Green beans cut in about 2" lengths
2 Tbsp Soy sauce
Salt to taste
1 Tsp Sugar
1 Tbsp Sherry or Chinese rice wine
1/3 c Stock or water
2 Tbsp Corn starch
3 Tbsp Water
3 Tbsp Oil
1 – 2 Tbsp Sesame seeds
2 Scallions minced or chopped in 1" pieces
1 Tbsp. Sesame oil

Blanch green beans in boiling water or steam until almost done. Set aside.

Mix second set of ingredients together and stir to dissolve sugar.

Mix cornstarch and water in a small bowl.

Heat oil on high heat to almost smoking in a wok or large pot. Stir in sesame seeds. As soon as they start popping, add scallions and stir over high heat 1 more minute. Add green beans. Stir to heat through.

Add sauce and lower heat. Simmer slowly 2-3 minutes.

Turn heat to back to high. Swish the cornstarch and water together and stir it rapidly into the beans to thicken the sauce.

Remove from heat. Stir in sesame oil. Serve.

Buca di Beppo Green Beans

Note: Using fresh beans and keeping them crisp during the prep are critical for this simple recipe to work.

1 pound fresh green beans
1/4 cup (1/2 stick) butter
2 medium lemons (juice)
Salt, to taste

Prepare the green beans by clipping off the stem end. Melt the butter in a saute pan on low heat. Squeeze the juice out of two medium-size lemons. Strain the pulp and the seeds out of the lemon juice. When butter is melted, carefully add the lemon juice to the pan. Raise the temperature to medium and reduce until the lemon juice and butter become a sauce. Do not brown the butter.Place the clipped, fresh green beans in boiling water for two to three minutes. Do not overcook. The green beans should remain crisp. Strain the green beans and add to the sauce in the sauté pan. Toss the green beans in the sauce and season with salt to taste. Serve immediately.

Garlic Beans

1 or 2 cans whole green beans
1 medium onion, sliced
5 cloves garlic, cut in half
1/2 cup granulated sugar
1 cup vinegar
1 cup vegetable oil
1/2 teaspoon salt

Drain beans; place in casserole with onion and garlic, mix . Sprinkle with sugar; let stand for 2 to 3 hours.

Blend remaining ingredients; pour over beans. Cover; refrigerate for 24 hours.

Drain before serving.

Green Beans Anyone Will Eat

How many of you know your green beans are good for you, but you just can't handle the smell. I love green beans, but before I can get them to my mouth the smell has strange effeect on my stomache. . So, we added a few things

2 cups green fresh beans,
2 strips bacon, cooked and chopped
1 tablespoon vanilla extract
2 tablespoons honey or white corn syrup
1/2 teaspoon garlic pepper

Put it all in a pot and cook on low till beans are done... and believe me, even the pickiest of eaters will eat these green beans.

Thia Green Papaya Salad

1 cup green cabbage, cubed into 2 inch pieces
2 cups green papaya, grated
1/2 pound string beans, clip tips and julienne
3 garlic cloves, minced
3 dried red chiles, chopped or 1 Tbsp dried Chili Flakes
1 tablespoon granulated sugar
3 tablespoons soy sauce
3 tablespoons lime juice
3 small tomatoes, cut into wedges
5 tablespoons peanuts, roasted and crushed
4 tablespoons cilantro leaves, chopped

Place green cabbage pieces on a large serving platter and arrange in layers the papaya and beans.

In a small bowl, mix together the garlic, chilies, sugar, soy sauce and lime juice.

Just before serving, pour the dressing over the salad and garnish with the tomatoes, peanuts and cilantro.

Gujerati (Green Beans)

1 pound fresh green beans
4 tablespoons vegetable oil
1 tablespoon black mustard seed
4 cloves garlic, peeled and finely chopped
1 hot red dried chile, crushed
1 teaspoon salt
1/2 teaspoon granulated sugar
Black pepper to taste

Trim the beans and cut into 1-inch lengths. Blanch by dropping them into a pot of boiling water and boiling rapidly for 3 to 4 minutes. Drain in a collander, rinse under cold running water and set aside.

Heat the oil in a large frying pan over medium heat. When hot, add mustard seeds. As soon as they begin to pop, add garlic and stir until lightly brown.

Add crushed red chile and stir for a few seconds. Add green beans, salt and sugar. Stir to mix. Serve

Savory Green Beans with Coconut

1/4 cup clarified Butter
1/2 cup flaked coconut
1/2 cup water
1 1/2 pounds green beans
1 medium onion, sliced
1 teaspoon ground coriander
1/2 teaspoon ground turmeric
1/2 teaspoon ground ginger
1 1/2 teaspoons salt

Prepare clarified butter (Ghee) Place coconut and water in blender container. Cover and blend on high speed until coconut is finely chopped, about 10 seconds. Cut beans lengthwise into halves; cut halves lengthwise into halves.

Cook and stir onion, coriander, turmeric and ginger in clarified butter (ghee) in 10-inch skillet over medium heat until onion is coated. Stir coconut mixture, beans and salt into onion mixture. Cover and cook over medium heat, stirring occasionally, until beans are tender, 20 to 30 minutes.

Almond - Cheese Green Beans

1 lb. fresh green beans, cut into 1 inch pieces
1/4 c. dry onion soup mix
1 c. water
3 tbsp. melted butter
1/3 c. toasted slivered almonds
3 tbsp. grated Parmesan cheese
1/2 tsp. paprika

Combine green beans, onion soup mix, and water. Cook over low heat until beans are tender. Drain. Spoon into serving dish. Stir in butter, almonds, and cheese. Sprinkle with paprika.

Green Beans with Almonds & Ginger

1 lb. green beans
1 tbsp. safflower oil
1 tsp. peeled, minced ginger root
1/2 tsp. tarragon vinegar
1/2 tsp. honey
1/4 c. sliced almonds

Mix together. Heat and serve.

"Another" Italian Green Beans

2 (10 oz.) pkgs. frozen Italian green beans or cut green beans
1/4 c. sliced almonds
1/4 c. butter
1/2 tsp. dried whole oregano

Cook beans according to package directions; drain. Saute almonds in butter until toasted. Add almonds and oregano to beans, stirring well.

Green Beans and Cauliflower with Almond Bread Crumbs

2 lbs. fresh cauliflower, separated into large florets
1 lb. fresh green beans, trimmed & cut into 2" lengths
Boiling salted water
2/3 c. bread crumbs
1/2 c. sliced almonds
1/2 c. butter

Cook vegetables in a large pot of boiling water 5 to 8 minutes until crisp tender. Drain and put into a large bowl. Keep warm. Heat butter in large skillet over medium heat 2 minutes or until golden brown. Stir in bread crumbs and almonds. Cook 3 to 5 minutes, stirring often, until nuts are lightly toasted. Add to hot vegetables, toss to coat.

Almond Chicken (Francais)

Ah, my old Friend Chicken!

8 oz. egg noodles
2 c. fresh green beans
1 c. sour cream or yogurt
1 c. mayonnese
1 c. dry white wine
1 tsp. salt
1 tsp. dried parsley flakes
1 tsp. dried dill
1/2 tsp. garlic powder
Dash pepper
1 c. croutons
1 c. grated Parmesan cheese
3 c. cubed, cooked chicken
1 c. sliced almonds

Cook noodles (if green beans are frozen, thaw but don't cook). In a medium bowl combine sour cream, Miayonnese , wine, salt, parsley, dill, garlic powder and pepper. In a 3 quart casserole (or 9 x 13 inch baking pan), layer 1/2 each of the noodles, green bean, chicken, croutons, almonds, cheese and yogurt mixture. Then repeat all layers. Bake, covered, at 350 degrees for 45 minutes or until heated through.

Green Beans Supreme

1/2 lb bacon, cut into 1 inch pieces
10 chopped green onions (including tops)
2 cloves garlic, pressed
1/2 lb mushrooms, sliced
3/4 cup blanched or slivered almonds
3/4 + 1/2 cup shredded Cheddar/Monterrey Jack cheese
1 cup sour cream
1 tablespoon white sugar
1/2 teaspoon salt
1 teaspoon dill weed
1 pound frozen petite whole green beans, steamed just until tender (can use fresh, or frozen cut beans)
2 cups onion flavored croutons
1 small can French fried onions

Stir together 3/4 cup cheese, sour cream, lemon juice, dill, sugar, and salt, set aside. Cook bacon pieces in frying pan until browned but not crisp, remove and drain on paper towels placed in the casserole dish you will be using. Saute onions, mushrooms, almonds, and garlic in reserved 3 tablespoons bacon grease. Remove from heat and add sour cream mixture. Add bacon, drained green beans, croutons and French fried onions. Wipe inside of casserole with the paper towel you drained the bacon on before removing. Spoon mixture into the greased casserole. Can be made a day ahead and refrigerated at this point.

Bake at 350°F for 25 to 30 minutes (a little longer if refrigerated).

Sprinkle with additional Cheddar/Jack cheese and return to oven just until cheese melted.

Green Bean Casserole and Dumplings

4 cans green beans, drained
2 cans cream of mushroom soup
1-2 cans mushrooms, drained
Bisquick baking mix
milk

Heat oven to 350°F.

Spray baking dish with cooking spray. Prepare dumplings according to box directions.

Drop by spoonfuls into baking dish. Set aside.

Mix together beans, mushrooms, soup and enough milk to make creamy. Spoon over dumplings.

Cover baking dish and bake at 350°F for 20 minutes or until dumplings are cooked through.

Bacon Wrapped Green Beans

Makes a delicious appetizer.
2 c. whole fresh green beans
Bacon to wrap beans
Russian dressing

Wrap 5 or 6 beans with half a bacon strip. Place side by side in baking dish. Pour Russian dressing over beans. Bake at 350 degrees for one hour or until bacon appears done.

Printed in the United States
By Bookmasters